SONGS OF PEACE

A. SPAROW

With love,
Anne ♡

i hope you find
some beauty here.

1.

love
sits with the lonely,
smiles to the sad,
holds hands with the hopeless,
looks to the least,
gives them the most,
builds up the bruised,
beautifies what it touches,
heals the sick,
softens the sharp,
binds up the wounded.

2.
lavender spills purple paint
& wandering petals over the hedge
of my garden where the quiet
spiders sit still,
fling art into nothingness,
& wait.
-the secret bravery of spiders

3.
she is
a wildfire blaze &
a wildflower song;
she will bloom in the ash
& set the wasteland free.

4.
someone once
said to me: "you
are too
gentle for
the world,
too soft—
a flower
to be
crushed
with the
weight of
wilderness."

but—
"kindness is
the wild in me—
softness is
the strength of
a thousand seas—
i will
bloom
for joy &
astonish the
desert with
color.
as for
the
terrible
world —
that's why i
stay soft."
-a rebuttal

5.
we are stained glass
souls trying
not to shatter;
mirth + color,
dirt + hope. . .

(roses plucked from colorful glass)
fragility + thorns,
but,
rainbows & redemption.

6.
you hold the
wonder of a world
wrapped in a heart-shaped
box. . .

(where the sea's sugar sand
frosts our feet)
& clouds
carry a bluebird sky.

7.
here is the collusion
of starlit petals & earth:
(seedlings root down deep in her soul). . .

. . . they will bloom
beauty from
her outstretched hands;
(those hands will scatter magic here)

8.
all butterflies are beauty;
winged jewels that hover
through breeze.
the world is wide enough
for them all to paint the sky:
sapphire, topaz, garnet, amethyst.
one's loveliness does not eclipse the other's.
us too—
we are beauty & the
world is wide enough for us all.
(we are enough)

9.

(i see you in my dreams)
of coral skies & crystal wolves
who howl songs
to starlight;
the world is
indigo,
fire,
opal,
violet,
alive:
(& i open my eyes)
& all goes grey.

10.
sit here
i am safe.
speak if you want,
or don't.
just sit.
let the hurt bleed from your bones,
breathe.
i will hold that
place in your heart
that is heavy.
-a friend

11.
to see beauty
is to see God's
heart beating.
(you are beauty, too.)

12.
weave the ribbons
through my hair &
wash my muddy feet—
"i will be your roots my dear,
& you, my wilderness."
i will dust your weary
wings & help you
dream again.
-mothers & daughters

13.
a wild orphan
of the night
(we poured her
drafts of
steady love)
& the stray cat
softened
(she seeks the
sun that cures the cold)
a corduroy paw
rests on my arm,
marigold eyes & a Cheshire grin
gleam in darkness as
(love displaces fear)

14.
in my pockets,
i have carried the
dust of a thousand places
(where lilacs climb
earth to emerald sea),
& i have learned:
it's all a gift.

15.
i am safe beneath
His feathers &
this Love will
forge my wings.
-fly

16.
we try
so hard
to tame the
wild things—
(—but why?)
we plant
concrete towers & tell trees
where to bloom:
(when
i wish we
would let the
wild things wild)
with
the creatures
that sing
in starlight
to the evergreens'
applause.

17.
she holds a candelabra
to the dragon
to discover why
he cries fire . . .

. . . be kind to the dragons;
be gentle with
their scales & their claws,

(because maybe—
the monsters bleed, too)

18.
when the world
weeps,
wrecks,
churns,
breaks,
bleeds,
burns:
don't
hide:
help.
helping heals.

19.
laced with
sun,
a rambling
field of
dandelions blooms
an oddly wrapped
meadow
of silver
& gold
(& every year
 they mow it down)
& every year
they rise again
(to mail our wishes
to the wind)
-persist

20.

let us be gentle to
all that we meet;
to the winter birds
& the snow-laced mice;
to the little deer
& the stray cat;
let us
light tangerine hope
in the winter;
its embers will
keep us warm
in the dark.

21.
there is no another,
only us in this
together.

22.

when you are afraid
(look at me); don't
look to the right or to the left;
don't look to the phantoms
fabricating fear in your mind;
(they aren't real) . . .

. . . i will cup your heart in my hands;
give you a gemstone sky to breathe;
(i will hold those fears for you)
let them fall now,
let them die.

23.
& i will wear these
thorns as a winter crown (they will
remind me that)
beauty's born from crimson pain.

24.
you,
the steady gardener
have carried
the roses
though their thorns
hurt your hands—
(you hurt your
hands for
me.)
—your love
has
made
my soul
bloom
the light of
a thousand stars.

25.
it's a simple saturday:
the sky blue: a perfect pale blue,
a hydrangea bloom blue,
the market below murmurs
with color & sound,
& while we might think
we are all stinging mad at the other,
here we are—
beautiful shades & shapes & sizes and dress &
memories & views—
here we are—
smiling at
the passing dogs,
examining tomatoes,
lending baskets,
holding doors,
laughing with
the littlest ones
laughing.

here we are—
strangers buying vegetables— out here in the wild
face to face
unclassified,
unlabeled,
here we are—
people collecting moments;
people savoring the breeze
on our shoulders;
people enjoying
 the colors of the earth,
people picking
sunflowers & bobbing balloons;
people sitting
at the great table
of the world;
people smiling
skyward & finding
imaginary
shapes
in the
traveling
clouds above.
-strangers

26.
be still
in storms
& rest in
rain—
you were
born to bloom
from pain.
-be brave

27.
braid the
moonlight
in your hair &
catch a crown
of stars
(run with the silver
creatures there);
let joy
color your
scars.

28.

do not apologize
for the tangles in your hair;
for the wild in your heart;
for the weeds in your garden;
for the cracks in your past;
for the makeup you forgot;
for the color in your thoughts;
for the magic in your words;
for the curve of your hips;
(never say sorry for the light
that makes all of you)
i promise, your light is enough.

29.
the arms
that hold
galaxies
(string starlight)
& carry oceans
carry you too
-do not fear

30.
we scratch the surface & beat against a current
to know: why do
we suffer?
broken people
break people &
we cause pain to fix it.
a mirror breaks,
opal glass skates over floor.
i pick up the pieces
that dance under & across & beyond—

— try to piece together
the answers,
but only find more questions glued to a great glimmer
of future hope.
why do we suffer:
sighing, settling, starving?
defeated, depressed, dying?
i have a broken mirror & blurry vision, but
i have a hand you can hold.
a safe place to sit.
an ear to listen.
breath to pray to God
who suffered, too.
i can't heal your pain, but
i can hold up the broken mirror,
look through the fragments darkly
& know —
that even shattered glass,
especially shattered glass,
best reflects the light.

31.

i dream of resting
my cheek in the gold
of a lion's coat,
weaving flowers
& wild grace
in his mane;
i dream of being still
with the lamb
in fields of
sea glass green
where unafraid birds
tumble magic
through the clouds:
don't you want to be
unafraid, too?

32.

the mad things,
the sad things,
the weary words,
the broken bits,
the painful places,
the tired pieces:
*all are working for
your good.*

33.
scattered wide by wild wind,
the acorns wait
(bury themselves
in silence)
until they bloom
where they fell:
deeply rooted.

34.
the stained glass
windows of autumn's
cathedral shake shards
of crimson, magenta, amber, orange
into sky where they shatter.
sometimes like the trees
we have to break a little
before becoming new.

35.
she walks in stardust;
gathers the moonbeams;
arranges a bouquet of
constellations;
she dances with
wolf & wildflower;
scatters the cherry blossoms
from the moon.
she's waiting for you there,
to plant stars in your hair;
to chase fireflies & hold your hand;
(to tell you)
she's never left you;
she's even with you now.

36.
the sun sits on
its porch pouring
the sky into strawberry
lemonade,
pulling the clouds into
saltwater taffy,
& breathing pastel peace
over all of us before
it dashes off to dream.
-a sunset

37.
it is harder
to trap a grudge
in your heart than it is
to set it free
(turn the key to the cage)
& let the bitter
things
f l y
from your bones.
(*& forgive*)

38.
a new day emerges
from a starry cloak
of night;
watch the rain
fall on rose-gold
leaves;
watch the rain glitter on
winter branches;
watch the trees open their
emerald umbrellas to the sky;
& watch them
drown the heavy things—
the dead things.
(watch the rain renew the world)

39.
consider the rose:
crushed velvet petals
unfurl in shades of
crimson, coral
salmon, cinnamon,
blush, ballet—
you can't force
it to bloom
in black & white.
-the importance of nuance

40.
do not be
fooled by her
softness, for
(you cannot contain
her)

she is the wilderness
of soft sage
& silver wolf
(shell pink & shades
of steel)

run with her, but
know:
you cannot
knock her down.

41.
do not be
afraid to cry—
your tears
will one day
water the
garden of
your deepest joy.

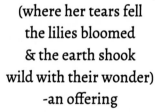

(where her tears fell
the lilies bloomed
& the earth shook
wild with their wonder)
-an offering

42.
a storm
stealthy creeps;
cloaked clouds &
slate streams
of rain—
the sky
boils fury &
you are afraid
but—
wrapped tight
in a blanket of stars,
another day
will dawn &
l o v e
suffocates
fear
-you are safe

43.
to the
tiny
chrysalis
clinging to mimosa trees—
you'll get there.
the good things
take their time.

44.
her heart—
a starry meadow
prisms pace
throughout her veins
-stardust

45.
the lights
spin on the seine
& my cinnamon hair
whips wild,
(you tuck the wisps
behind my ear)
& shield me
from the shout
of winter wind
(i take your
hand—
it's warm)
we walk the gilded bridge
into another world.
(i'm not going
to have you
forever, but i
will hold on to
you now)

46.
i don't do
small talk
very well—
how do you answer "how are you?"
when—
your heart
blooms
to a wildflower
rhythm—
your soul
sings
the salt-air of
an ocean
song—
your arms
embrace
a meadow
of stars—
"i'm good, i guess"—
"how are you?"

47.
i want to be where
the phones are
dim & the fireflies
are bright.
-escape

48.
if we all have stars inside
our bones (we hide some of them in cages for)—
we are afraid of what our light can do—

let's unlock the galaxies from our fingertips,
— (our magic is needed here)

49.
forgiveness is a door,
& on the other side—
freedom.
-let it fly

50.
i want to be a scavenger of
light (collect it from the broken stars)
melt it back together into marigold streams;
watch it make the shadows golden.

51.
the snow
geese tremble on the
frigid sea & dew frosts the dirt
(january mornings
peel the skin off
of new beginnings). . .

suddenly, the sky's door
swings wide in color;
(apricot for joy;
lavender for peace;
cinnamon for love);

& silver for new hope that
drizzles a spark over
the earth.

52.
we whispered our dandelion
prayers to the wind . . .

trust that we can release
the answers to the sky;
(they don't belong to us)

53.
the wild Atlantic's daughter:
she wove a gown of sequins
that were given by the sea;

the seagulls' hymns remind her
that here, she can just . . .

be.

54.
seek the light
when you can.
watch it
warm the mountain daisies
& notice—

all need a crack to let the light in—
aren't we a little broken, too?
we can let the
light heal
what's hurt in us.
(our weeping isn't wasted)
& pain is a pathway
for the light to
sift through—to spill over,
out, & eventually—into others.
what's broken becomes our beauty.

55.
we walk the winter beach
(the wind is ice & the
water glows emerald-blue-beyond)
the seagulls shine silver
& i stop my stride:
hundreds of broken shells—
fragments of a former life
(orchid, opal, moonstone, linen)
tumble in the tide,
are washed new in the tide
when i realize—
there is hope for the broken things.

56.
love unravels
then transforms.
soothes chaos
to peace,
crushes condemnation
to ashes,
sets the dust dazzling
beauty,
*sends death
dashing backwards*

57.
exhale the
starlight:
(wrap the sunflower sky
around your shoulders) . . .

it's a joy to be alive;
alive for the moon to kiss your hair;
(to hear the seabirds
swish silver wings)
to hear the ocean whistle
peace . . .
shhu, shhu, shhu

58.
love walks, talks,
teaches, reaches,
moves, serves,
gives, forgives,
bends backwards,
breaks with the broken,
spills over messy,
but never, ever fails.
-a definition

59.
you taught me to
plant the pain;
"everything grows back," you said,
"but not in the way you expect."

you taught me that wounds let the light in
& that tears water the ground where the
wildflowers grow;

& that one day, bruises will bloom in lupine &
lavender,
& broken bones will stand
silver as aspen trees.

60.
she wears the sea
inside her soul
(the waves carry her free);
she plants a garden
of falling stars
(& brings its
light to me).

61.

let's agree to be
healers in
a world wrecked by war;
a wild ocean
of kindness
that batters
bastions
of hurt, of hate—
let's agree to
do for one person
what we wish we could
do for all people—
& that will be the difference.

62.
i have lived
a straight line
to the
sea since
i was born—
& what has
always
astonished me:
the soft sand
on the shore
never ceases
to whisper
to the waves
no matter
how angry
they are.

63.
the moon's magic
is her resilience
to bloom
through the bleak.
she gives her
strength to
the dark &
always burns
back
brighter.

64.
do you hear it?
(the light, awakened);
the resurgence of the wildflower;
can you feel the earth's
heart beat faster?
soon we will untangle
the frozen stars from
their strings
& watch the moon
grin on more
colorful days.

65.
here is our table.
silver tree bark &
peeling paint
work worn & ragged—
knots etch our stories, hear our smiles,
catch our tears.
we meet here:
pull up rickety chairs & sit
sip coffee, break bread—

— listen to our days' stories,
come as we are—
a place is set for all of us:
a napkin, cream, sugar, a porcelain mug.
we belong, talk, listen,
understand, welcome—
transform.
here is our table.
doesn't look like much but
tired wood whispers our lifetimes
& all are welcome here.

66.
a snowfall of butterflies
will land inside my ribs;
their wings kiss my forehead &
starlings tangle sun in my hair;
(what a beautiful world it is)
when you are here.

67.
the poetess
(a lioness)
brave & blazing bright—
she stalks
the twilight wood for words
to give the world light.

68.
hatred—(poisons veins & floods our brittle skin
with ash)
& division—(dices us up to spill us out hollow)
how then
can we fix us?
(because we are breaking)
—& wielding
wrath as
a weapon
puts power in
hatred's
hands—

(let's take hate's hands,
& hold them tight.)
from this,
hope will rise.

69.
even the magnolia
takes a break from
blooming now & then
(you can stay still for as long as you need)
the falling petals are beautiful, too.

70.
hold my hand
so that the scarlet pain stills,
(hold it as the crimson ebbs
& flows)
trace constellations over my
scars & tell me that
when the night's flames bleed
into violet,
the morning is coming.

71.
your embrace
planted a lavender
sky in my heart
(will you take my hand
in Provence fields?)
& the sun will rain honey
for days.
-lavender & honey

72.
do you remember the year
the roses didn't grow?
we cried our pain into the
dirt & broke the
ground with our sorrow.
it's been 5 years now,
& we dream of summer,
a summer when the wild roses will bloom,
& on a silent night,
a Child
will crush
the thorns to
bring us
beauty.

73.
to the
winter rose
(all ruby and milk)
that holds the heavy
snow—
(your bare arms
tremble)
you carry so much—
it's okay to
let go.

74.
light splashes
through the sidewalk
cracks of my heart
& paint splatters fuchsia
on my fingers; new beginnings
rise with the sun;
(& thus begins the
dissolution of the dark).

75.
darling—
perfectionism
is a cage
(forgive your crooked wings)
see the shore embrace
uneven tide
(let's love all
the broken things)

76.

release the things you
do not need; release the
ones that are not for you;
watch them fall as pastel
snowflakes; watch them melt
screaming color to peace.

77.

it's magic out there now . . .
the tree lights drip frozen glitter
over the wooden nativity,
& so we gave Mary a
crown of evergreen;
she clasps her hands
over her heart
to treasure
wonder, (thrill), grace;
over her heart to carry
a promise of tomorrow—

— Hope lifted on
a monarch's wings
into an azure sky.

78.
be gentle to
every thing alive;
let kindness be your courage
(read the earth's colors
& let beauty bleed into your
soul)—

—so that you can find
magic
in every blade
of grass,
magic
in every freesia petal,
so that you can find
(magic in everything).

79.
go my dear &
dust that dream,
the one you've tucked
beneath bright wings
(the one they say is
just mad) . . .

. . . you don't bloom for them

so,

go—

80.
miracles prevail in
the tiny things:
steam curling from a coffee cup,
iridescent feathers,
a rainbow of soap suds,
snow in the sun,
a black cat dancing,
butterflies in my hair,
a fox's tangerine laugh,
violets that shimmer on the
windowsill,
& the way your hand curves soft around mine.

81.
she adorns
reindeer with daisies
as they gallop
through her dream
(do you see
the sparrows
in her hair?)
"she knows this can't
be real,"
they say,
"but that doesn't
change a thing."
-imagine

82.
over & over,
let us bloom
from what is dead in us;

(let our colors resurrect
from the ruin)

83.
she has a swallow tattoo
to remind her of home;
rooms of cobalt bricks &
salt water dreams:
(gardens of coral, twilight seas, & indigo lace)
she combs the shells through her hair,
washes her sandy feet,
(& pretends she never has to leave).

84.
i watch your
hands weave a garden
of stars
slowly,
patiently,
perfectly—
it may take centuries for them
to align, you say—
& so i learned not
to despise the
unhurried things.

85.
i held a mountain's
hand today
(it was soft yet i was stone)
he whispers he'll carry
the sky for me
(& that i'll never walk alone)

86.
be kind to your
body:
your lines & stripes & scars & curves:

be kind to your
lioness heart,
your tired eyes,
your wildflower soul,
your messy hair,
your muddy feet:

love all of it
like every glittering
grain of you
holds eternity.

87.
once we found a broken bird
flung from obsidian sky

(we pieced a splint
from popsicle sticks
in hopes that
it would fly)

& so it is with our own wings
we break just to be born—
we are all fractured in some way
(be gentle with our thorns)

88.
there is a space
between the sidewalks
(you left it there yourself)
but it's empty just the same;
i will kiss the little
scar on your cheek &
promise: if you let
the light in,
the primroses will rise from
the pavement.

89.
we crush the lavender
to soothe our scars
& peace runs through our veins —

if your broken heart could heal
one's pain—
would you let it break?
-a question

90.
to me & the hummingbird
(thrumming jade-joy)
in the winter seeking warmth:
you tell us,
"come";
you cradle us
by poinsettia fire;
we were unexpected,
but you
became our
home.

91.
a lily won't
linger for
approval—
she shakes the mud
& blooms to bloom.

92.
even a crow's feathers
look like a rainbow
in the right light.

93.
there's a field
of wildflowers
in your heart

(don't be afraid to
wear it on your sleeve)

94.
the lights
are dancing colors in Rome
& i am lost in the
wonder of turquoise & copper wishes.
how many desires fly breathless
in these iridescent waters?
contentment rests
on the
paper wings
(that do not flap at all).

95.
she wore
a yellow dress
& pushed a wheelbarrow
of stars
(she ran wild
with the wolves)
& knew every wildflower by name
-an epitaph

96.
today i saw an angel smile.
her plum cheeks
folded into
lovely lines
like a paper crane
(& she laughed the
light of a hundred suns)

i may never feel cold again.

97.
you are serenity.
a shade of blue:
a sapphire sea,
a primrose petal,
a robin's egg.

(you breathe peace into my bones
& still my red rose heart.)

98.
once i met a girl who
wore tulips in her hair
(she labored long to
plant the seeds
she thought could
cure despair)

she never saw a barren field
(only possibility)
& so she harvests the stars that
color the dark & climb
a ladder to sea.

99.
there's glitter in
her bones & yellow
fire in her hair—

(perhaps she
is a comet glowing
in the frosty air?)

she is possibility
(like watercolor sky)
she breathes dragons from
the indigo clouds
(& teaches them to fly)

100.

watch the copper dragonfly
(hum patina & light)
swim for joy in a
sea of blush carnations;
(watch her deliver greetings
from another world)

101.
take me to the forests of your mind
(lay me among your maple thoughts)
i am so happy to stay here,
to dwell in wild & wonder,
(to taste wildflowers & sunlight)
you are the most beautiful
place i have ever been.

102.
it's okay to
make some room.

(even the sky lets go
of the stars)

& it is beautiful to watch them fly.

103.
a kaleidoscope
of petals
will teach us:
how beautiful
the fragile ones
are.

104.
beautiful are the women
(bearing life from the dirt)
who kiss the seeds that
awaken the earth (who grow the
roots that paint color & light)

how beautiful are the ones who give life.

105.
forgive us,
for we are
messy
(beautiful)
creatures.

106.
i tell you that
i'm afraid to take these thorns
from my wound, for they
have hidden the ache inside.

you hold my sadness in your arms,
collect my tears in a bottle
(you count every one that
falls)

& like an alchemist,
you melt my leaden tears to gold;
you promise me they will
soften the thorns where they fall.

107.
she pressed the sand dollar
white into her palm.

"a treasure," she said.

she traced the porcelain
star & its scalloped edges.

she tossed it to
sea where it tumbled soft
in the sand.

"why?" i asked.

"because treasures don't
belong in
glass jars."

108.
a deluge of stardust
swirled
upon a lonely field,
& from its
broken glitter,
we built a miracle.

109.
breathe color
into our winter bones
(& apricity into our lungs),

may we dance a rainbow
tonight &
exhale the sun.

110.
hope is the
bird that flew
from its cage into
the palm of God;

hope is the sunrise
of rose-gold light
(before, we never opened
our eyes);

*hope is the surprise of
second chances.*

111.
you cannot move
a mountain in a day;

watch the blue velvet
river wrap round it;

watch it knit the
sediment into coral lace, steel lace;

watch it weave debris
to dance under the stars of 1,000 midnights;

watch & learn: the mountain doesn't
move until the river does.

112.
come & let your brittle
feathers rest.

(the air is heavy & you've
carried so much to the sun)

the sky will sing over you
& the clouds will hum
a pastel lullaby.

come & let your
weary wings heal,

you will fly again very soon.

113.
i wish there was a name for
(that blue);

the blue that paints
my bones the color
where sky & sea meet;

(the blue of poppy petals
& shades of peace)

the color i feel when
i am free.

114.
to the
blackbird singing
fragile hope
to turquoise stars
do not fear
(tonight could be the night)
that you move the universe.

115.
scatter my identity
beneath the dirt;
let it sing unseen with
secret roots; let it stretch
into pale blossoms to live,
& then,
(lay me among the dying petals)
& here i will bloom again.

116.
the fireflies
sing outside the jar now.
(watch their freedom decorate
the sky);

you let them go even though
you didn't want to lose their
light,
& that is courage.

117.
let us learn to love as the
wild geese know
(when you fall, i fall)
& *i will never leave you.*

118.
you can find her
by the sea
(maybe in the poppy fields);

do you see her
painting
lipstick on the
dandelion's wishes?

(she is unfurled stardust)
a lioness with
wild hair, dirty feet,
and bluebird dreams.
she brings you adventure,
& you will never stop loving her.

119.
let's find where
the panther waltzes peace
with the sparrow,
(& let's dwell among
the wildflowers there).

120.
the
sky slips
indigo over the
row homes: apricot & lilac;
she lines her days with
hyacinths & hope—knowing,
soon winter falls
back to
sleep.

121.
one day you
will find gratitude
for the things that
gave you pain.
broken people
may break people
but you,
you will be okay.
you will plant that
pain & harvest
peace where
the wild roses grow.
(& one day you will
realize, it was
all a gift)

122.
tuck the lipstick away
in your little blue purse;

string pink roses in your lavender hair
& dance tonight;

dance over the shattered bones
of your broken fears;

you are free now;
you are unafraid.

123.
they carried the colors on opal
wings
& built a nest of light;
prisms race from out of the storm
(& songs of peace ignite)
-the doves

124.
we sent you paper lanterns into
twilight's breath;
did you see them, racing to
the stars' doorstep?
you sent us snow-laced butterflies,
yellow origami wings;
tiny, fragile miracles,
folded with love,
as if you never left.

125.
do not be afraid to go slowly.
the moon carries
time on her silver shoulders
& even she knows:
she cannot be made whole in just
one night.

126.
i have given up on growing thick skin,
(for i want to feel the ocean soak my bones);
i want to feel the colors that don't exist;
(i want to feel it all)
& i know that people will hurt me, but
(there is a meadow on my sleeve)
& it will bloom anyway.

127.
the roots dig deep
from our ribs;
stem through our veins;
pulse blush & lavender
petals (into our wildflower hearts)
for we are wonderfully made

128.
here is my door
(with an azalea wreath)
& it is open to (the stray dog)
& the orphaned deer;
(to the blind cat) &
her butterscotch kittens; (to the lost sparrow)
& the outcast souls—
(here is my door; it is open wide)
to all the starving creatures—
come in.

129.
the sky must get so tired,
holding stardust & storms,
swirling sapphire & blush,
shifting moods & changing days
(i used to wonder why it turned
grey)
but now, i think i understand.

130.
storms & constellations swim under your
skin & sometimes you feel that the sea
inside
swells too big for a heart (that can be held
in your hands);
exhale the stars, the rain, (all of it);
rest your bright wings (for you are alive) &
it is okay to feel it all.

131.
ashes will fly on indigo wings
(passion flowers bloom mauve
from the mud); the lioness
stalks colors lost in the void;
(we die when we forget to see)
—beauty can
be our redemption.

132.
look at how the sun dances
on your skin,
*& do not for a second
doubt your wonder*

133.
she was a lovely ache
like everything else that's truly
beautiful; & so she left with wild
moonlight
tangled in her hair; (she left with
cherry blossoms stained on her
feet),
& she knew that there were better
things ahead of her (for she was
beginning to believe in) the magic
inside of her own skin.

134.
you can be the softness
of a summer petal
(shell pink & indigo stems)

you can be the wild
of a tigress heart
(black glitter & ochre stars)

(it's a lie) *that you have
to choose*
(one or the other).

135.
we are all branches
of the same tree
(& some of us are)
digging for stardust in our
pockets
to scatter through the night.

136.

milky lace swims on the sea's skin
(weaving patterns over my shoulders)
& i know we are wonder;
we can breathe, feel, move, run, & (we
can break the chains) that tether us to
rusty piers.

137.
i want to crawl inside your
arms (a hearthstone of gardenias &
sapphire wings)—your hands write
this magic
inside of my heart (your hands hold
everything that
is beautiful)—which is Love.

i pray you found
peace here.

love,
anne

a special thanks
to the artists:
Molly Sue Design Co.
Createthecut.com
Papersphinx
Paula Kim Studio
Aqwacolor
Origins Digital Curio
Paperly Studio
Passion PNG Creation
Tinkerco Digital
Watercolour Clip Art
The Willow Wood Studio
Lisa Glanz
Blue Eyed Henri
Carrie Stephens Art

CPSIA information can be obtained
at www.ICGtesting.com
Printed in the USA
FFOW03n1207220218
45201054-45755FF